SUPERLEEDS

CONTENTS

2-5	MY DREAM DEBUT SEASON	MICHAEL BRIDGES
6-7	OLLY PUZZLED OVER FRENCH SUPREMACY	OLIVIER DACOURT
8-9	GARY MAKES KIDS FEEL AT HOME	GARY KELLY
10	TRIVIA QUIZ	
11	LEE BOWYER POSTER	
12-13	WORLD CUP WINNERS WILL COME FROM OUT OF AFRICA	LUCAS RADEBE
14-15	HARRY'S TOO HOT TO HANDLE	HARRY KEWELL
16-17	LEEDS LEGENDS	GILES, DAY, HUNTER, STRACHAN
18	ODD FACTS 1	
19	JONATHAN WOODGATE POSTER	
20-21	BAKKE LIVES UP TO O'LEARY PREDICTION	EIRIK BAKKE
22-23	SIX OF THE BEST LEEDS V BESIKTAS	
24-25	DREAM START FOR STEPHEN	STEPHEN McPHAIL
26	SPOT THE EURO GROUNDS	
27	JASON WILCOX POSTER	
28-29	LEEDS LEGENDS	MADELEY, JORDAN, COOPER, CHARLES
30	ODD FACTS 2	
31	ALAN SMITH POSTER	
32-33	1992 CHAMPIONSHIP	
34-35	DRAGON SET TO ROAR	MATTHEW JONES
36	QUIZ	
37	DOMINIC MATTEO POSTER	
38-39	PLAY LIKE SMITHY!	
40-43	VIDUKA LIKES MAKING HIS MARK	MARK VIDUKA
44	QUIZ	
45	IAN HARTE POSTER	
46-47	FUTURE IN GOOD HANDS	
48	QUIZ ANSWERS	

PRODUCED FOR LEEDS UNITED PUBLISHING LTD.

by GOSNAYS SPORTS AGENCY AND POLAR GROUP, LEICESTER.

Editor RICHARD COOMBER

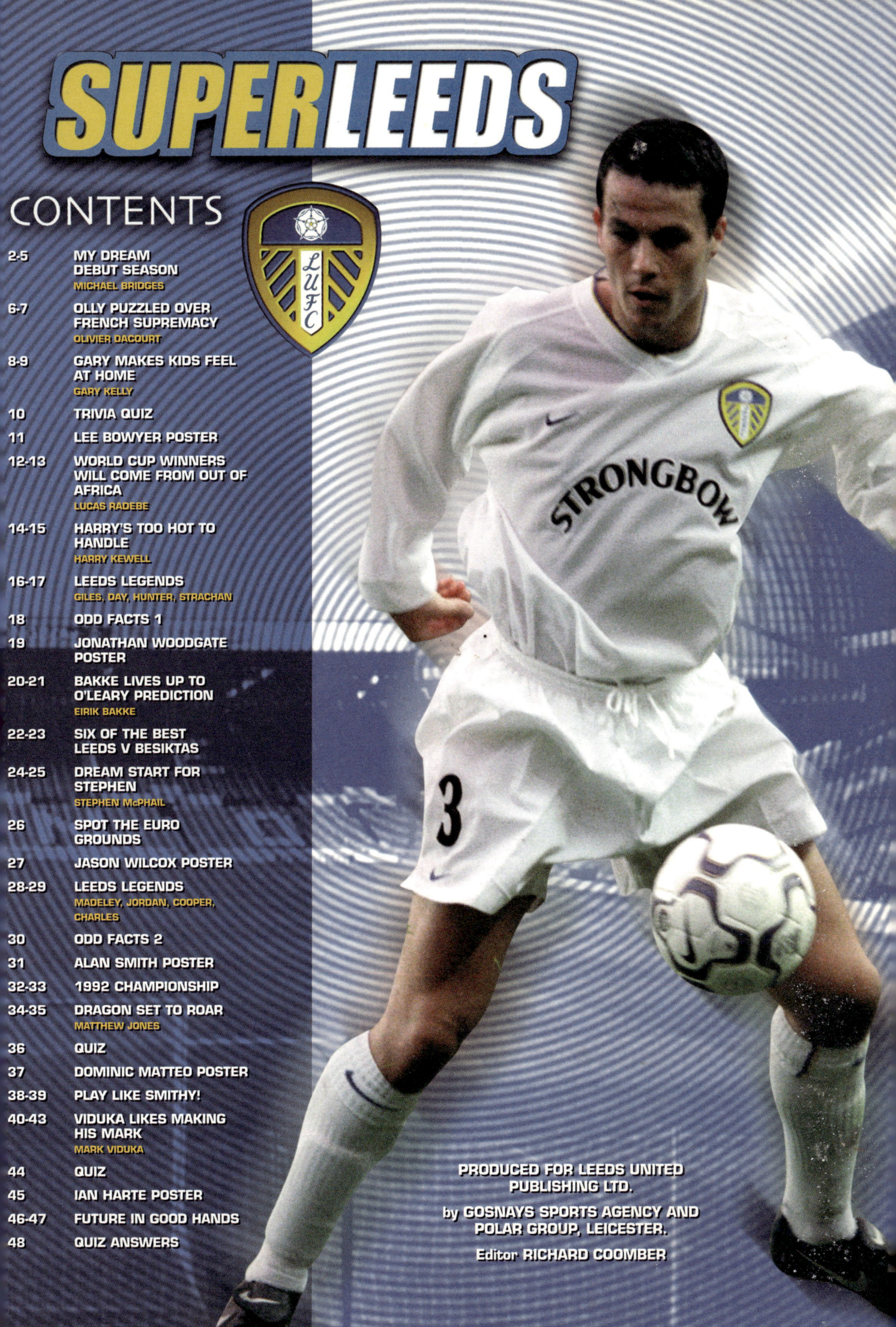

My Dream Debut Season

Michael Bridges believes his dream debut season with Leeds United helped him mature as a footballer and as a person.

The striker arrived from Sunderland in a £5 million deal in the summer of 1999 as the then club record signing.

Jimmy Hasselbaink left shortly after Bridgey's arrival in a dispute over wages and that left the new boy under pressure to deliver the goals.

However he rose to the task superbly to net 21 goals for United in a season which saw them finish third in the Premiership and reach the semi-final of the UEFA Cup.

And Michael recognises the importance of grabbing a hat-trick at Southampton in only his second game for United.

He said: "Scoring a hat-trick down there got the fans on my side quite quickly so it was very important.

"It took the pressure off. I scored 21 goals but that was nothing compared to what the team achieved. This is the best team this club has had for a while.

"Jimmy left before the season started which made me think 'I am going to be thrown in at the deep end here'. I had to learn to swim fast. It was a very steep learning curve."

Bridgey started his career with Sunderland after having been spotted by legendary north east talent scout Jack Hixon.

Hixon is the man who also spotted former England captain Alan Shearer when he was a teenager and helped propel him to the very top of the game.

Shearer also became a mentor for Michael with the pair regularly in contact and the Leeds striker keen to pick the brains of his Newcastle counterpart.

Michael harboured hopes of partnering Shearer in the England attack but the latter's retirement

FACT-FILE:

Born: August 5, 1978.
Position: Forward.
Leeds Debut: Derby County (Aug 7, 1999). Elland Rd - Leeds drew 0-0.
Former clubs: Sunderland.
International: England Under-21 international.

"I learned so much in that first year and am still learning now. I think I grew up as a player and as a guy in general."

from international games ended those hopes.

Bridgey's debut season in the Premiership could not have gone any better and has left Leeds fans wondering why he was so far down the pecking order at former club Sunderland.

Michael became a popular player at the Stadium of Light but due to the superb partnership of Niall Quinn and Kevin Phillips, he often had to be content with a place on the bench.

So when Leeds came in for the England Under-21 international, he jumped at the chance to move south and says he has never regretted the decision.

He said: "Last season was a great start for me personally. I was nervous when I first came but I settled down after the Southampton game.

SL 2000 PAGE 3

"I learned so much in that first year and am still learning now. I think I grew up as a player and as a guy in general.

"Coming down here and leaving home was a good step for me because it has helped me develop both on and off the field.

"There is always pressure in football. I was supposed to be going to Tottenham when I left Sunderland but instead I came here. It has been a steep learning curve but one I have enjoyed.

"The great thing at Leeds is anyone will score goals in this team because we have so many players with ability in the team.

"We create a lot of chances as a team. People ask me about the highlight of my first season but to be honest the highlight was the whole season

"The two goals I scored out in Russia against Lokomotiv Moscow were memorable though. It was my first European away tie, so it was especially memorable.

"The first one was a crossed ball to Lee Bowyer at the far post, he headed it back across and I put it in. The second came when Eirik Bakke put me through.

"The last day of the season was pretty special too because we found out we were in the Champions League. That was a great moment."

The biggest disappointment from Bridgey's debut season came with the UEFA Cup elimination against eventual winners Galatasaray.

United lost the first leg 2-0 in Istanbul just 24 hours after the death of two Leeds supporters in Turkey when everyone involved with the club, including the players,

My Dream Debut Season

had difficulty thinking about football.

The return leg a fortnight later at Elland Road was an emotional affair but despite Eirik Bakke scoring twice, the Turkish club forced a 2-2 draw to go through on aggregate.

Bridgey missed a good chance for United in the second half of the first leg and admitted: "If I had scored over there I think it would have changed the whole tie.

"The annoying thing is Galatasaray are not as good as Roma and we beat the Italians.

"Galatasaray have some very good individuals, but we should have beaten them. To be so near to a European final and miss out was heartbreaking but we've got a lot of experience under our belts now and it will stand us in good stead."

Bridgey's tally of goals was a superb testament to his ability and helped Leeds cement their place as one of English football's big clubs.

His form did, however, fluctuate across the season but his importance to the side was illustrated by these dips coinciding with a poor run of results for United.

He said: "We started off really well, then had a sticky patch over Christmas, bounced back again and were flying. Then everything started to go wrong.

"The Galatasaray incident didn't help, of course, and confidence hit rock bottom. We hadn't lost our ability but when you lose confidence the chances don't go in.

"At the start I had loads of ups, then I had a few downs and came back with some ups. It was great to qualify for the Champions League."

SL 2000   PAGE 5

Olly puzzled over

Ask Leeds United's French midfielder Olivier Dacourt why his country is so strong at international level and he thinks for a while, shrugs his shoulders and admits to being baffled.

The talented midfielder believes we in England have some of the best football academies in Europe for young players to develop their skills - and managers like United's own David O'Leary are quicker to give those youngsters their chance at first team level than they are in France.

Dacourt also insists the atmosphere inside English grounds motivates players into giving 90 minutes' effort in every game - part of the reason he decided to play in this country in the first place.

Record transfer

'Olly' spent a season with Everton where he collected too many yellow and red cards for his own good, but his disciplinary problems failed to end his love affair with the English game and after returning to France for a spell with Lens, he signed for Leeds in a club record £7.2million deal in mid May.

Recalling his early days in France, Dacourt said: "Football was my hobby when I was a child. It's hard to remember the early years

FACT-FILE:

Born: 25 September 1974 in Montreuil, France
Position: Midfielder
Height: 5ft 9in
Joined Leeds Utd from Lens, June 2000, for £7.2m
Squad Number: 4
Leeds debut: 9 August 2000, against 1860 Munich at Elland Road (Champions League qualifier) W 2-1
Previous clubs: 97-98 Strasbourg, 98-99 Everton (£4m), 99-00 Lens (£6.5m)
Quote: "I could have gone to Italy or Spain but I don't like their football as much. I love everything about English football. There is always a great atmosphere and the stadiums are full."
Odd fact: Olly had a poor disciplinary record at Everton but was only sent off once - against Leeds United!

PAGE 6 SL 2000

French supremacy

but at 13 I joined Strasbourg, which meant living 600 kilometres from my parents' home.

"I spent ten years with Strasbourg and at 16 I was in their first team, but that's unusual. It is better in England when you are young because in France it is very difficult to force your way into the first team of a big club before you are 20.

"I don't know why French football is so good when there are not many opportunities for young players. We have a lot of naturally gifted players back home but the top clubs don't have the best soccer schools. We have some clubs like Auxerre, Nantes, Strasbourg and Lens who work just to create a good player and sell him to the really big clubs.

"So the smaller clubs in France are going to be in big trouble if the transfer system is abolished. It will be even worse in England because you have so many clubs over here who depend on transfer fees from the big clubs to stay in business."

Home of football

Dacourt says playing in the English Premiership is a major attraction to French players. He explains: "I think English crowds show more passion. There are some clubs with passionate crowds in France, but nothing like you have here. After all, England is the home of football and attendances are very high. That was one of the things that attracted me to come and play here.

"When I was young I enjoyed watching English football on TV. The fans make so much noise and most of them stick to supporting one team all their lives. It is like a religion."

Olivier has quickly settled in as a first team regular at Leeds where his infectious sense of humour has made him a popular player in the dressing room. His English is all the better for spending that season at Everton, though there isn't a trace of Scouse in his accent!

United's players have even picked up a few French phrases and love to try them out on Olly during breaks in training. "The players here all get on so well, the club has a wonderful academy and there are many more good young players than you would find at any club in France," he says.

So it seems there are parts of our game which are better than you'll find across the channel. Yet, as Kevin Keegan so often pointed out, there are so many foreign players in the Premiership these days that our international team is bound to suffer.

"The players here all get on so well, the club has a wonderful academy and there are many more good young players than you would find at any club in France."

Gary Makes Kids Feel At Home

Joining Leeds' Academy is something every young United fan dreams of. It is the first step on the road to running out at Elland Road in front of 40,000 fans with the likes of Ian Harte, Harry Kewell and Alan Smith all having started off as part of United's youth set-up.

Moving away from home for the first time can, however, be difficult for young lads because they have to leave behind family and friends.

United full back Gary Kelly knows all about that and readily remembers how homesick he was on first arriving in Leeds from Ireland ten years ago.

He said: "When I think back to how near I came to going back to Ireland in the early days, it is just incredible how things have turned round for me.

"I was ready to go home but (then Leeds boss) Howard Wilkinson persuaded me to stay, switched me to right back and everything has happened from that.

"Most people from Ireland are from big, close families. I was the only one out of thirteen who came away from home.

"It's an eye opener to come to a different part of the world, not have your friends there any more and have to start from scratch. It took me a long time to settle. I still miss home even now."

Kelly is now a vital part of the Leeds side and last season he received a huge accolade from his fellow pro's - being selected at right back in the PFA team of the year.

However it is not just out on the pitch where Gary sees his role at Elland Road.

The 26-year-old uses his experience of moving away from home to help the Irish lads to settle after joining Leeds' Academy.

He said: "I know what the young lads are going through and like to look out for them. You can look at them some mornings and know they are missing home.

"It gets you so you can't eat or do anything for thinking of your family and friends back home.

"I see it in some of the lads who have come across the Irish Sea. I try to help them settle and I love doing it.

"At their age it is nice to know there is someone here who knows what they are going through and can help them to cope."

Kells is a wonderful role-model for any youngster starting out in the game with his level-headed manner and wicked sense of humour making him one of the most popular in the dressing room.

It is a role he is determined to live up to as he remembers how he

FACT-FILE:

Born: July 9, 1974.
Position: Defender.
Leeds Debut: October 8, 1991. Home to Scunthorpe United in a 3-0 win in Rumbelows Cup.
Former clubs: None.
International: Full Republic of Ireland international.

was helped by senior players such as Gordon Strachan, David O'Leary and Nigel Worthington as he settled in Leeds.

He said: "I would never have stayed in English football if Howard Wilkinson hadn't told me I could give my family whatever they wanted if I stayed in the game and did well here.

"Howard knew all about my home sickness problem and after our chat I remember ringing home and crying down the phone as I told my family what he had said.

"I owe so much to Howard Wilkinson not only for giving me my chance and having that chat, but also for making sure I had the right role models taking me under their wing.

"I understand what the young lads are going through and look out for them."

SL 2000 PAGE 9

TRIVIA Challenge

1. Which English club did Olivier Dacourt play for before Lens?
2. Who were the two Leeds players who took part in Euro 2000 last summer?
3. Which Scottish team did Mark Viduka join Leeds from in a £6 million deal?
4. Who was the Leeds captain when United last won the league title in 1992?
5. Which London club did David O'Leary play for before joining Leeds, initially as a player, in 1993?
6. Which former Manchester United star is now in charge of the Leeds' Academy?
7. How many points did United win last season when they finished third in the Premiership?
8. Which United player made his debut for the Republic of Ireland in May 2000?
9. Who scored Leeds' first ever goal in the Champions' League this season?
10. Who did former Leeds midfielder Alfie Haaland join for £2.5 million in the summer?

YOU CAN FIND THE ANSWERS TO THIS AND ALL THE OTHER QUIZZES ON PAGE 48!

PAGE 10 SL 2000

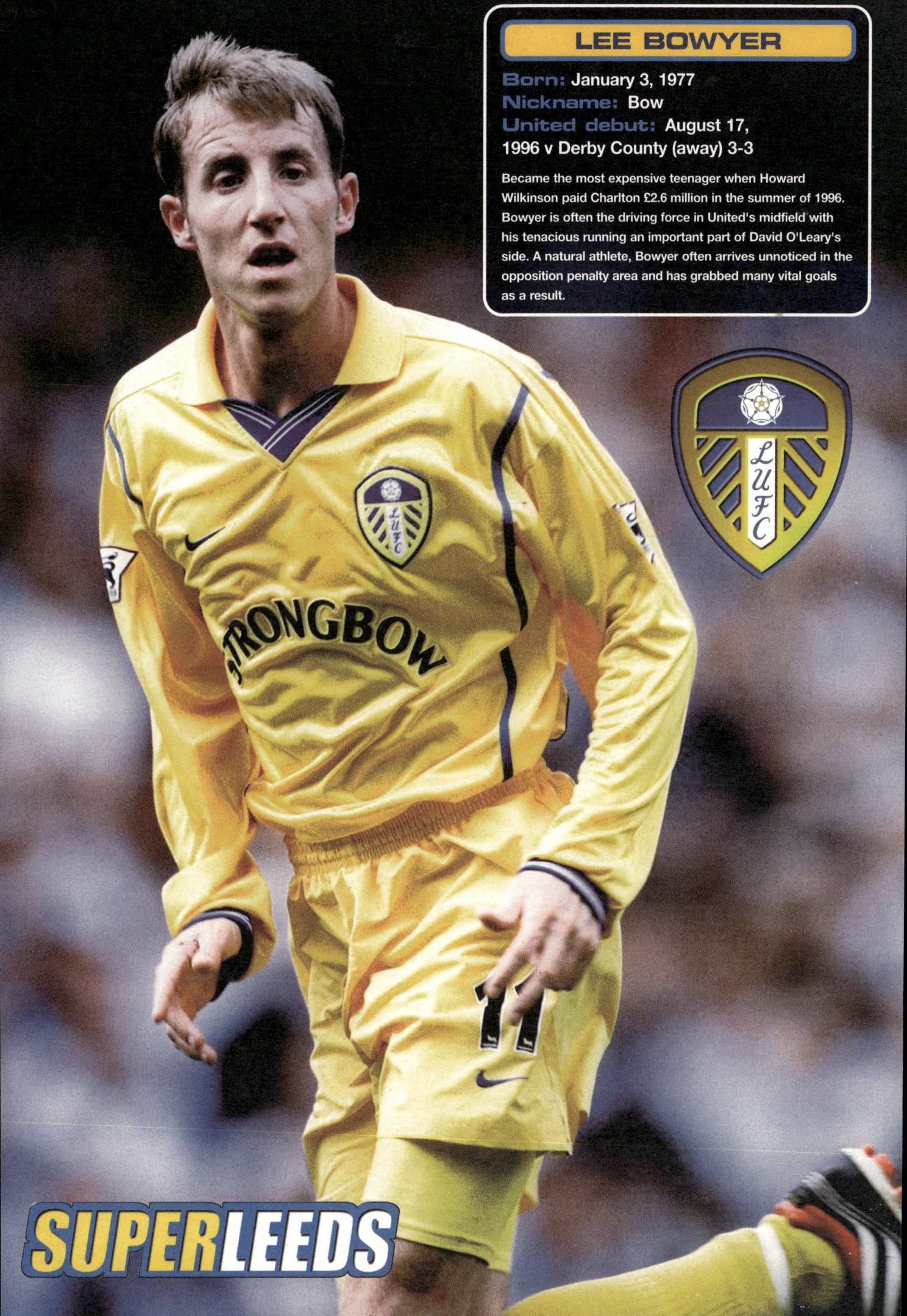

LEE BOWYER

Born: January 3, 1977
Nickname: Bow
United debut: August 17, 1996 v Derby County (away) 3-3

Became the most expensive teenager when Howard Wilkinson paid Charlton £2.6 million in the summer of 1996. Bowyer is often the driving force in United's midfield with his tenacious running an important part of David O'Leary's side. A natural athlete, Bowyer often arrives unnoticed in the opposition penalty area and has grabbed many vital goals as a result.

SUPERLEEDS

World Cup Winners will come from Out of Africa

The world's greatest footballer, Pele, once predicted that an African country would win the World Cup before the end of the 20th century.

The great Brazilian was not correct but the massive improvement in standards in African football over the last ten years or so, suggests it won't be too long before that vast continent can boast the winners of football's greatest prize.

We have seen countries like Cameroon, Nigeria and Morocco emerge as world-class teams. Liberia produced World Player of the Year George Weah. And an increasing number of major stars are emerging from South Africa, including Leeds' skipper Lucas Radebe.

When Lucas joined Leeds from Kaizer Chiefs in 1994, South Africa were rated 74th in the world, having shot up from 109th the year before. At the start of the new century they are joint 22nd alongside Scotland.

It's a remarkable improvement for a country who were banned from international football until 1991 because of the racist apartheid regime that used to be in force in that country, preventing black citizens having the same rights as white.

Lucas can take a great deal of credit for his part in South Africa's emergence, with his contribution as a player, captain and ambassador for his native land.

He has led them to African Nations Cup success at their first attempt and perhaps his proudest international moment was to lead out the team when 'Bafana Bafana' made their first-ever World Cup finals appearance in France 1998.

"It's very emotional to pull on the South African shirt," Lucas admits. "You realise that you are representing the whole country, the new South Africa. You start to think of your brothers who never got the opportunity, think about your family who are back home watching you, the people ... you get goose bumps and it gets very emotional."

At 31, Lucas still has many more years left to contribute to the growth of Leeds United into a major European power at club level but he already knows what he wants to do when he finally hangs up his boots.

He is such a hero in South Africa that he could probably walk into any job he wanted, in or out of football, but his ambitions lie with the grass roots of the game, with young footballers. It would be a natural follow-on to the voluntary work Lucas already does in South Africa for SOS Children's Villages, a charity which helps orphaned, abandoned and destitute children.

He explains: "I want to work with the children back home and help develop their talent. There are

PAGE 12 SL 2000

lots of exciting youngsters but we need more experienced coaches to guide them.

"The success we have had over the last few years has raised interest and expectations, and I think in years to come, we shall have a team that can challenge for the major honours in world football."

One concern he has is that club football in South Africa is not developing as fast as the international scene, so the best young players, like Manchester United's Quentin Fortune, are having to follow Lucas to Europe to earn their living.

"The main problem is sponsorship. Some clubs have big sponsorships but some don't have any at all and that's the problem. The government and companies need to get involved and build the league up. All the best players are going abroad because there is not enough money in the clubs.

"That's a shame but perhaps as the economy grows we will be able to change that and have a league with all our most talented players in it, though I'm sure many will want to test themselves in Europe at some stage in their career."

Leeds fans are just delighted that Lucas was one of the pioneers for his country in English football and hope he picks up many trophies for United in Europe before heading for his exciting mission back home.

Harry's Too Hot To Handle

Harry Kewell is a player who every Premiership manager would want in his side.

The Australian has emerged as one of the hottest talents around with seasoned observers queuing up to lavish praise on H's shoulders.

Former England bosses Terry Venables and Bobby Robson have seen almost everything in their long coaching careers but both men admit to being blown away by Harry's skill and pace.

The current season looked like being the one where Harry would truly become a world star by taking both the Olympics and the Champions League by storm.

However as we all know, H's season has been decimated by an Achilles injury which eventually required surgery and is expected to keep him out until after Christmas.

Any team would miss a player of Harry's calibre and as well as United have done in his absence, every Leeds fan cannot wait until he pulls on the famous white shirt again.

There are few sights more guaranteed to get the Elland Road fans to their feet than Harry in full flight.

His pace, skill and strength make him one of the most dangerous footballers around. We all have friends who support other Premiership teams and even if they are critical of Leeds, 'H' is always someone who they agree would be worth a place in their side. When a player is out for a lengthy period of

Hot To Handle

time, doubts often surface about how effective they will be on their return. Few Leeds fans hold such fears about 'H'.

You only have to look at someone like Roy Keane to realise how much of a force a player can be after recovering from a bad injury.

The Manchester United skipper missed nine months after being injured in his side's 1-0 defeat at Elland Road in 1997. Keane's absence from the Manchester United side played a huge part in them surrendering the Premiership title to Arsenal.

There were fears about the impact Keane's injury would have on such a fine player but he has proved since then his standing as arguably the best central midfielder in England.

Harry was deservedly voted the PFA's Young Player of the Year last season with Keane claiming the main prize. 'H' also picked up United's Player of the Year with Newcastle boss Bobby Robson saying: "He is an attraction wherever he plays.

"He is extremely elusive, he can work on both sides, he's got his change of pace which allows defenders to think they have got him, and off he goes again.

"He's got a wizard of an eye and a great shot. Top player."

Terry Venables had H as one of his star players during his time in charge of the Australian national side.

Venables said before Harry was struck down by injury: "He has all the attributes to be an outstanding player - he's got a great left foot, he's good in the air and he can shoot, cross and score goals.

"He's got pace and he's not afraid of the physical side of the game either."

Robson and Venables are two of the wisest men involved in football over the past 20 years and here opinions count for a lot. They know a good player when they see one.

And that is why Leeds fans are counting the days until they can see 'H' terrifying opposition defences once again.

Well

SL 2000 PAGE 15

Leeds Legends

Johnny Giles:

Like Strachan, Johnny Giles arrived at Elland Road from Manchester United to play a leading role in transforming Leeds into title winners. Giles was the complete midfielder and went on to play more than 500 games for Leeds, scoring 115 goals. His partnership with Billy Bremner was the foundation on which Leeds' success was founded in the 1960s and 1970s. He was a member of the United side which were very unlucky to lose the 1975 European Cup final 2-0 to Bayern Munich. Is now working in journalism.

Mervyn Day:

Signed from Aston Villa for a bargain £30,000 in February 1985, Day went on to become a hugely popular player during what were often difficult times for United. He was United's first choice goalkeeper for the next five seasons and played a huge part in the revival of the club during the promotion success of 1990. Day also helped United to the semi-final of the FA Cup in 1987 only for Coventry to deny Leeds a trip to Wembley. Day was also in goal when United reached the Second Division play-off final in the same season only to lose in extra time to Charlton.

PAGE 16 SL 2000

Norman Hunter:

One of the fiercest competitors to play for Leeds, no collection of United legends would be complete without Norman 'Bite Yer Legs' Hunter. He joined Leeds from school and made his debut in 1962 before going on to become an integral part of the great Don Revie side which brought so many trophies to Elland Road. He featured in all of United's Cup Final appearances between 1965 and 1975 and was voted Player of the Year by his fellow pro's in 1973.

Gordon Strachan:

The driving force behind Leeds' First and Second Division championship successes in the early 1990s. Strachan joined Leeds from Manchester United for £300,000 in March 1989 and proved to be Howard Wilkinson's most astute signing. His great skill, determination and dedication acted as an inspiration as Leeds won promotion in 1990 and 12 months later he was named the Footballer of the Year. However Strachan's crowning moment came in 1992 when he skippered United to the league title. Also went on to be awarded the OBE in 1993 before joining the coaching set-up at Coventry City.

DID YOU KNOW?
ODD UNITED FACTS THAT ARE STRANGE BUT TRUE

FOOTBALL IN THE CITY

Supporters who visit Elland Road these days may find chanting 'There's only one United' second nature.

But it could all have been so different with all of us now cheering on 'City' instead of 'United' in the Premiership.

Leeds United were formally elected to the Football League on May 31, 1920, but that was only after a club called Leeds City had been expelled eight games into the previous season.

City were suspended and eventually kicked out of the Football League after an astonishing scandal involving illegal payments made during World War I.

The punishment came as an almighty shock to everyone in Leeds with even an offer by the Lord Mayor to take charge of the club in place of the discredited directors failing to save the club.

Burslem Port Vale were instead admitted into the league in place of the Leeds club and took over City's remaining fixtures in the 1919-20 season.

City's playing staff were duly auctioned off to the highest bidder with the entire squad fetching just £10,000.

Football had been a late starter in Leeds due to the popularity of rugby in the area. However Leeds City were formed in 1904 and entered the West Yorkshire League, moving into Elland Road in October after Holbeck Rugby Club disbanded.

The club's first season in the Football League was 1905-06 and they finished sixth. The expulsion of City then paved the way for United to be formed and the rest, as they say, is history.

First off the bench

The first substitute to appear from the bench for United was Rod Johnson who replaced Jack Charlton in the 2-0 win over Aston Villa at Elland Road on September 1, 1965. Before the introduction of substitutes in the 1965-66 season, teams who had a player injured were forced to play with ten men for the rest of the game.

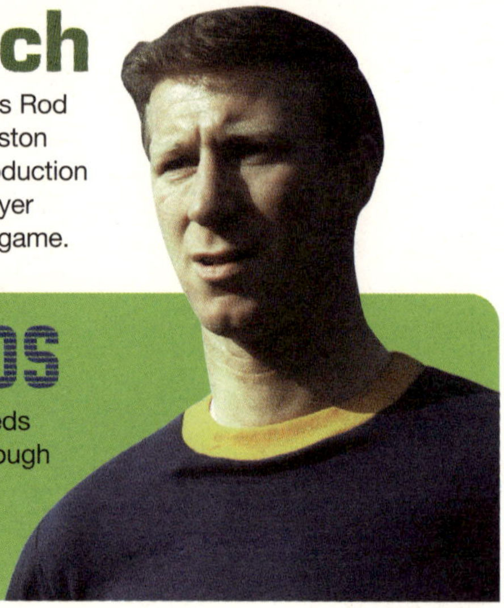

APPEARANCE RECORDS

Jack Charlton and Billy Bremner both appeared for Leeds United a staggering 773 times during their careers although Billy's total includes one substitute appearance. Jack, meanwhile, started every game he took part in and he netted 96 goals while Billy finished with 115.

McCall played for Leeds

Bradford City captain Stuart McCall is a vivid illustration of just why the Bantams pulled off their successful bid to avoid relegation last season.

The Scotland international joined City aged just 16 and after spells with Everton and Rangers, returned to Valley Parade in 1998 to help guide the club to promotion and then survival in the top flight with his battling displays a big influence.

Then Leeds boss Billy Bremner was interested in signing McCall in the late 1980s but the flame-haired midfielder chose Merseyside instead.

However did you know that Stuart's dad Andy played over 60 games for United in the 1950s? Andy was an inside forward born in Scotland who joined United from West Bromwich Albion in August 1952 and left three years later.

Stuart may be 100 per cent committed to Bradford now but as a youngster he was a big Leeds fan and travelled all over the country watching United.

RECORD CROWDS

The record attendance at Elland Road is the 57,892 which packed in to watch United's FA Cup fifth round replay clash with Sunderland in March 1967 which finished 1-1. United won the second replay 2-1 but crashed out against Chelsea in the semi-finals. The largest crowd for a league game is 56,796 which watched a goalless draw with Arsenal in the old First Division in 1930.

Deadly Gentle Giant

The legendary John Charles holds the record for hat-tricks in his Leeds career with 11.

The Gentle Giant had two spells with United and is recognised as the best Leeds player outside of the great Don Revie side of the 1960s and 1970s. The Welsh international enjoyed a phenomenal 1953 with no less than five hat-tricks for United.

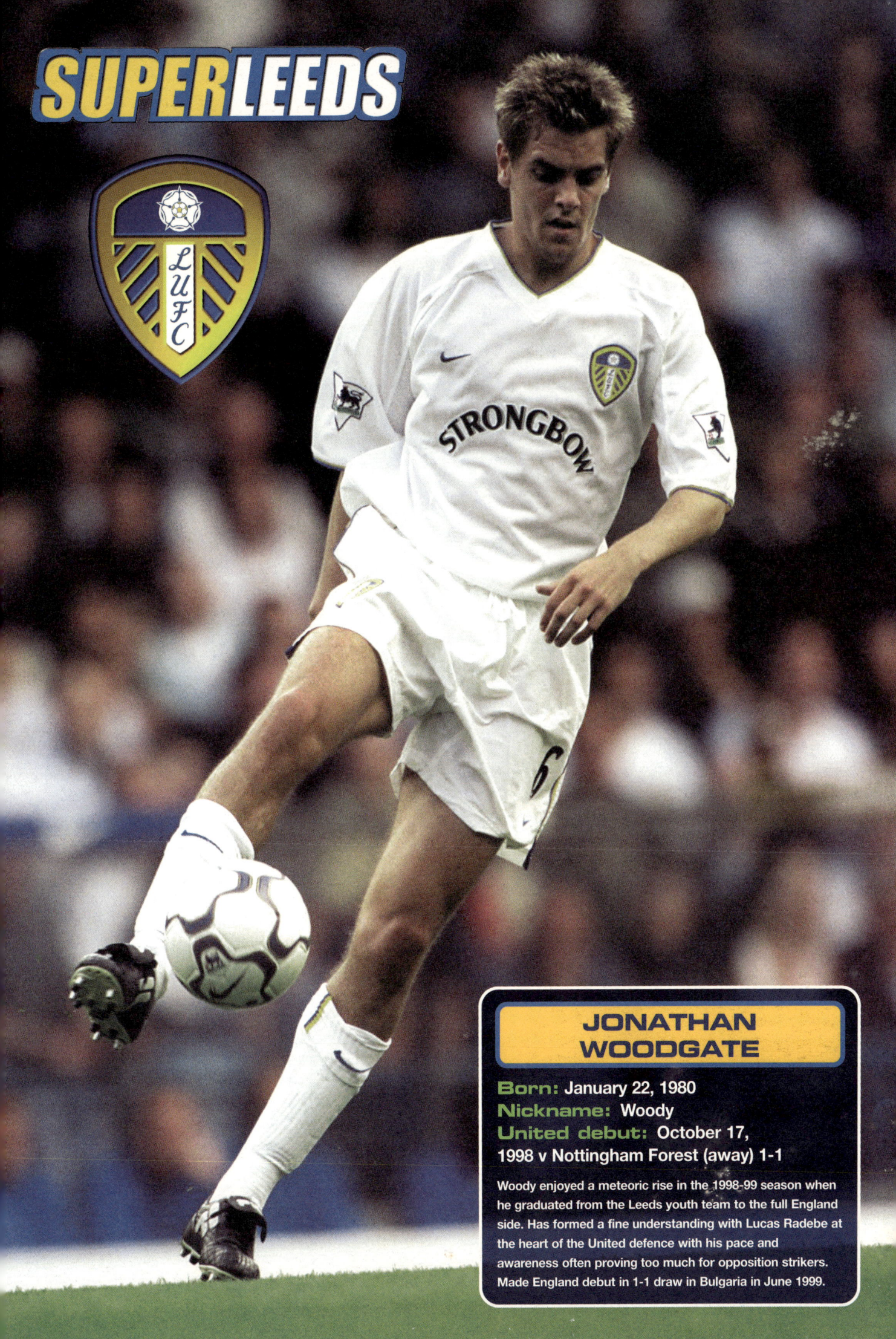

SUPERLEEDS

JONATHAN WOODGATE

Born: January 22, 1980
Nickname: Woody
United debut: October 17, 1998 v Nottingham Forest (away) 1-1

Woody enjoyed a meteoric rise in the 1998-99 season when he graduated from the Leeds youth team to the full England side. Has formed a fine understanding with Lucas Radebe at the heart of the United defence with his pace and awareness often proving too much for opposition strikers. Made England debut in 1-1 draw in Bulgaria in June 1999.

best Leeds United bargain he would surely pick out Eirik Bakke.

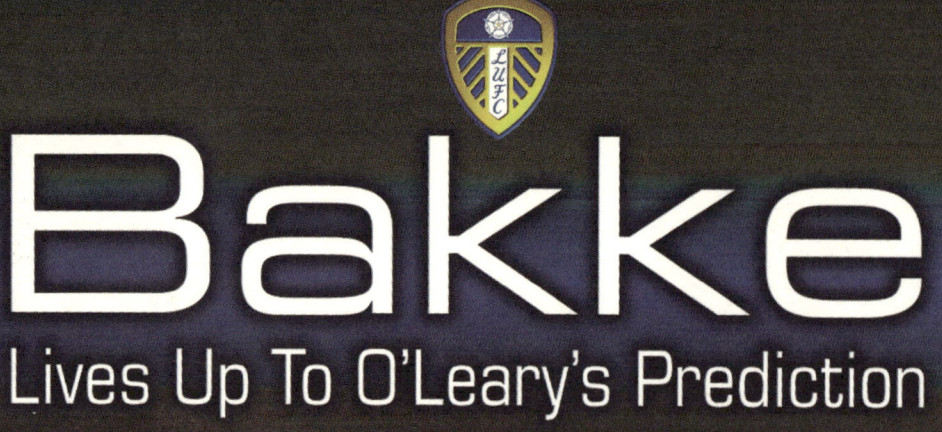

Bakke
Lives Up To O'Leary's Prediction

Signed for £1,750,000 from Sogndal in May, 1999, the Norwegian international was a revelation last season. His excellent form while savouring his first Premiership season earned him a place in Norway's squad for Euro 2000, and although the Norwegians failed to progress beyond the first stage, Eirik started two games and also made a substitute appearance.

He settled so comfortably into United's midfield that O'Leary said: "I am so pleased that my chairman trusted me when I told him what a good player Eirik is. Before buying him from Sogndal I said to the chairman: 'We have a lad here who we can develop into a top quality player'. That is exactly what Eirik has become."

Unfortunately, Bakke made a stop-start opening to the new season. He was sent off in the home Champions League qualifier against TSV 1860 Munich and, after figuring in a 2-0 home win against Everton, suspension cost him his place in the away leg against Munich.

He returned for the 2-1 win at Middlesbrough only to suffer an ankle injury which was slow to mend. Yet he showed last season that he has the ability and drive to be one of the Premiership's most effective midfielders - whether tracking back to help out his defence or bursting forward to make his presence felt in the opposition's penalty box.

Eirik is particularly effective at set-pieces, giving the side additional options when Ian Harte decides the angles are too tight to attempt those sledgehammer free kicks.

Eight goals in his first season represented a good return for the Norwegian, who collected four of his goals in the FA Cup, two in the UEFA Cup and two in the Premiership. He scored his first two goals for the club in a 2-0 FA Cup victory against Port Vale at Elland Road - but many Leeds fans missed them. Only 11,912 spectators turned up for the third round tie, which was played on a Sunday afternoon, after Vale's directors rejected United's attempt to reduce admission prices. The club's lowest FA Cup crowd, incidentally, was 10,144 against Bournemouth as long ago as 1939.

Eirik's next goal also came in the FA Cup, an eighth minute effort at Maine Road sparking a 5-2 victory after Shaun Goater had given City a shock lead as early as the second minute.

By then, Eirik was firmly established as a first choice member of the midfield and scored for the third successive round when United lost 3-2 at Aston Villa at the fifth round stage. David O'Leary's team led twice but Benito Carbone proved the scourge of United's defence with a memorable hat-trick.

It was not until Wimbledon arrived at Elland Road in March that Eirik broke his Premiership scoring 'duck' but he did so at the double in a 4-1 win. Then Galatasaray were on the receiving end of another Bakke brace in a 2-2 draw at Elland Road in the UEFA Cup semi-final, second leg, though it wasn't enough to prevent the Turks from reaching the final.

FACT-FILE:
Born: 13 September 1977 in Sogndal, Norway.
Position: Midfielder.
Leeds Debut: 11 August 1999, against Southampton away (Premiership) W 3-0
Former clubs: Sogndal

"We need a big squad when we are involved in so many competitions, so most of us will have a part to play at some stage."

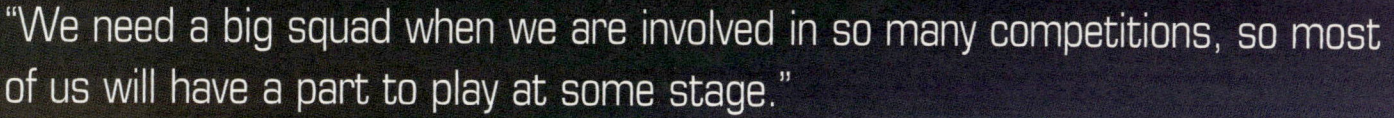

Bakke's father, Svein, was a star striker at Sogndal where he piled up 320 goals, but Eirik's worth to the team is measured more in terms of determination, skill on the ball and effort than goalscoring.

Eirik says: "The great thing about the squad of players at Leeds is that everyone puts the team first. We accept it's a squad game and the manager can't pick everyone in the team. We need a big squad when we are involved in so many competitions, so most of us will have a part to play at some stage."

Eirik was especially grateful to his fellow Norwegians Alfie Haaland and Tommy Knarvik for making him feel so welcome when he first arrived in England. Another Norwegian, Gunnar Halle, left to join Bradford City soon after Bakke's arrival and Haaland and Knarvik have since left the club too.

"They helped me settle in and it was good to have them around," said Eirik who was sorry when Alfie was left out of Norway's squad for Euro 2000.

"I enjoyed playing in the finals in France, even though we didn't go beyond the first stage," said Eirik. "We finished with the same number of points as Yugoslavia, who went through to the quarter-finals, but we didn't score enough goals."

Now Eirik is hoping for further international honours, though his priority is to enjoy an injury-free spell with United and maintain the rapid progress that made him one of the best newcomers to the Premiership last season.

SIX OF THE BEST

UEFA Champions League, Tuesday 26th September 2000

Mark Viduka could hardly have wished for a better return to Elland Road from the Olympics than the six-goal mauling United inflicted on Besiktas. Viduka's first competitive goal since joining United from Celtic in a £6million move sparked off the goal rush, Lee Bowyer started and finished the rout with goals in the seventh and 90th minutes, and Eirik Bakke and substitute Darren Huckerby jubilantly joined in.

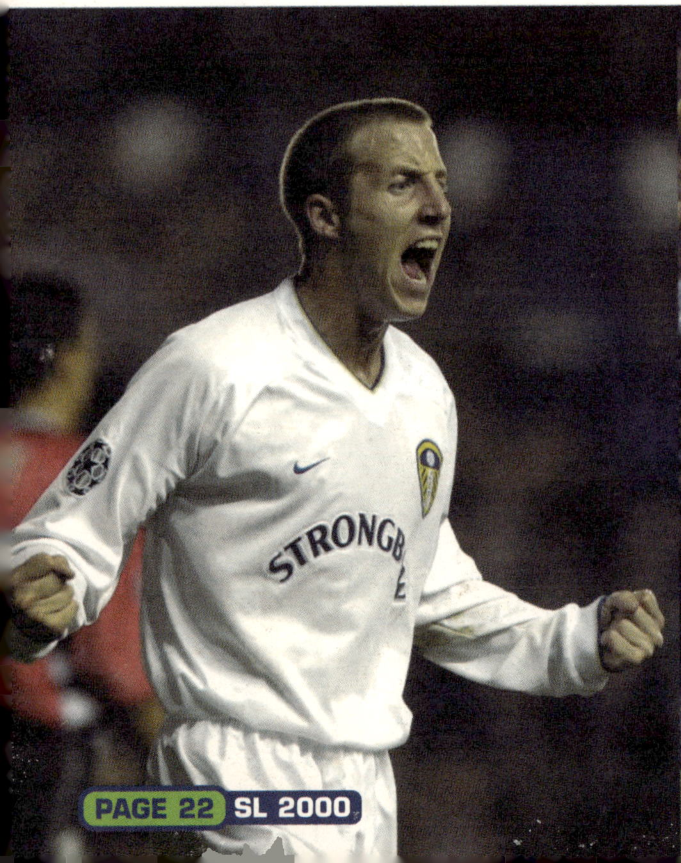

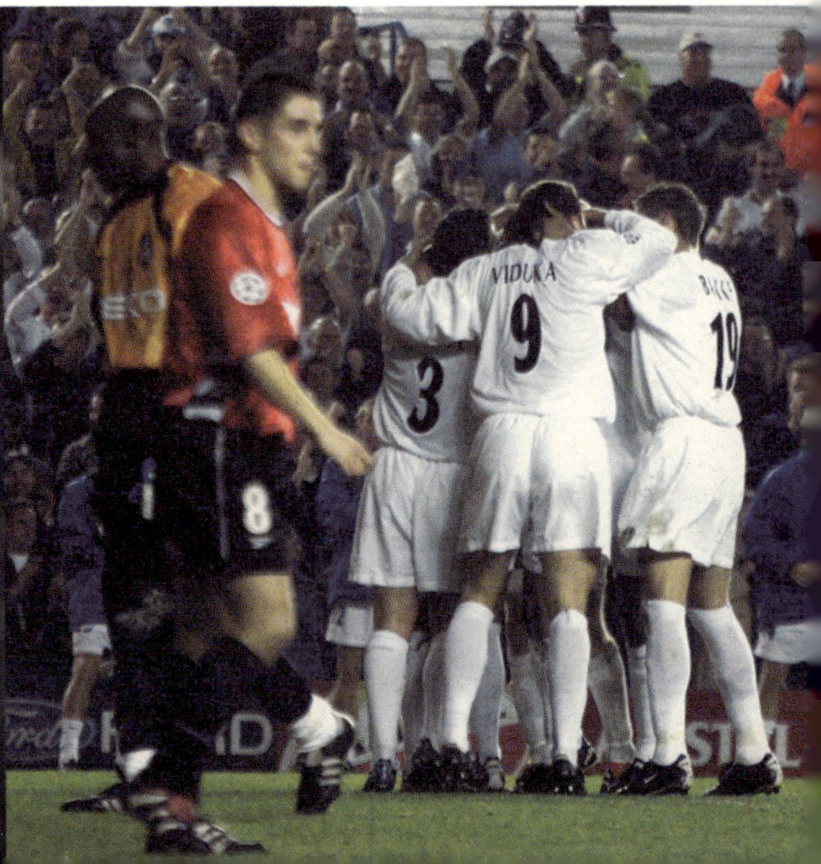

At a time when most of his Leeds team-mates were setting off on their summer holidays, Stephen McPhail was realising a boyhood dream.

Dream

FACT-FILE:

Born: December 9, 1979. London.
Position: Midfield.
Leeds Debut: Substitute v Leicester City on Feb 7, 1998. Leeds lost 1-0.
Former clubs: None.
International: Full Republic of Ireland international.

PAGE 24 SL 2000

After working his way through the schoolboy, youth and Under-21 international set-ups, McPhail finally won his first full cap for the Republic of Ireland.

And the talented United midfielder then followed that with his first international goal in early June when the Republic beat South Africa 2-1.

He said: "I was delighted with how the summer started. Making my debut seemed a long time in coming because I had to pull out of a few squads due to injury.

"But it finally arrived when we played Scotland at Lansdowne Road. Everything went all right and it was just a shame we didn't win."

Mick McCarthy's squad flew out to America just a few days after the clash with Scotland to take part in the US Cup.

McPhail retained his place in the side to face the USA and responded by setting up the opening goal for Watford's Dominic Foley.

And then when the Republic of Ireland faced a South African side which did not feature Lucas Radebe who was out having an operation, he curled a corner straight into the net.

Macca said: "It was a great feeling to score. The heat had been making me feel a bit dizzy but then the goal came just before half-time.

"I was just happy to see it go in - I can't really describe the feeling.

"The first few corners I had taken before that had caused a few problems so I was just

Start
For Stephen

looking to curl it in under the crossbar for Niall Quinn to try and nod the ball home.

"The keeper was just catching them on the line so I curled it in and it flew over the keeper and into the far corner."

Macca was actually born in London before being brought up in Dublin where he went on to play for the Home Farm club which has also produced Gary Kelly and Ian Harte.

However when he was approaching his fifth birthday, Macca was taken to live in New York where his father had a job.

He lived in the New York borough, the Bronx, for three and a half years before returning to Dublin.

And the fact he lived out in America made scoring his first goal over the Atlantic even more special.

He said: "There was a big contingent of Irish fans there. All my dad's family live out there and were at the game so that made it extra special."

SPOT THE EURO GROUNDS

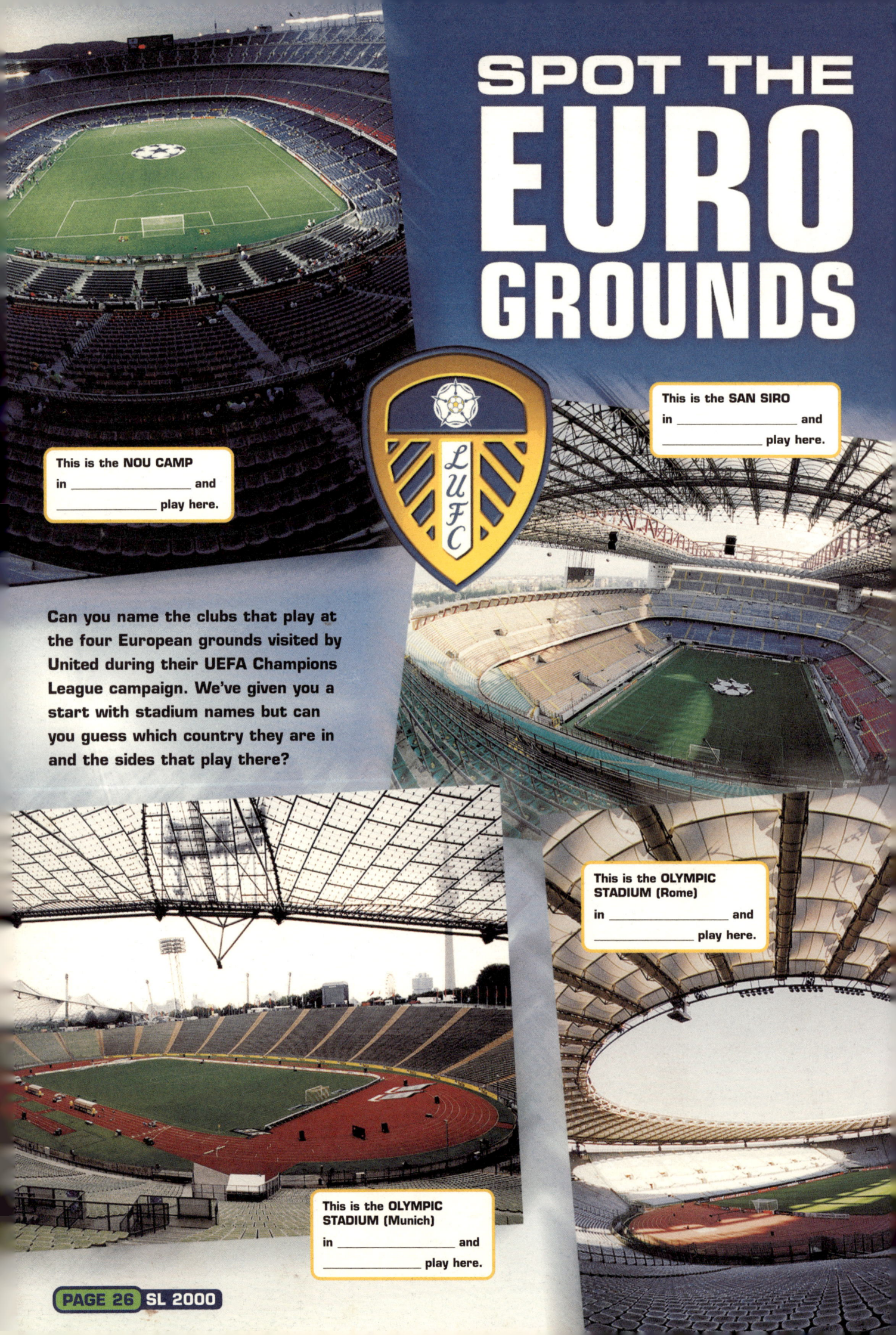

This is the NOU CAMP
in _____ and
_____ play here.

This is the SAN SIRO
in _____ and
_____ play here.

Can you name the clubs that play at the four European grounds visited by United during their UEFA Champions League campaign. We've given you a start with stadium names but can you guess which country they are in and the sides that play there?

This is the OLYMPIC STADIUM (Rome)
in _____ and
_____ play here.

This is the OLYMPIC STADIUM (Munich)
in _____ and
_____ play here.

PAGE 26 SL 2000

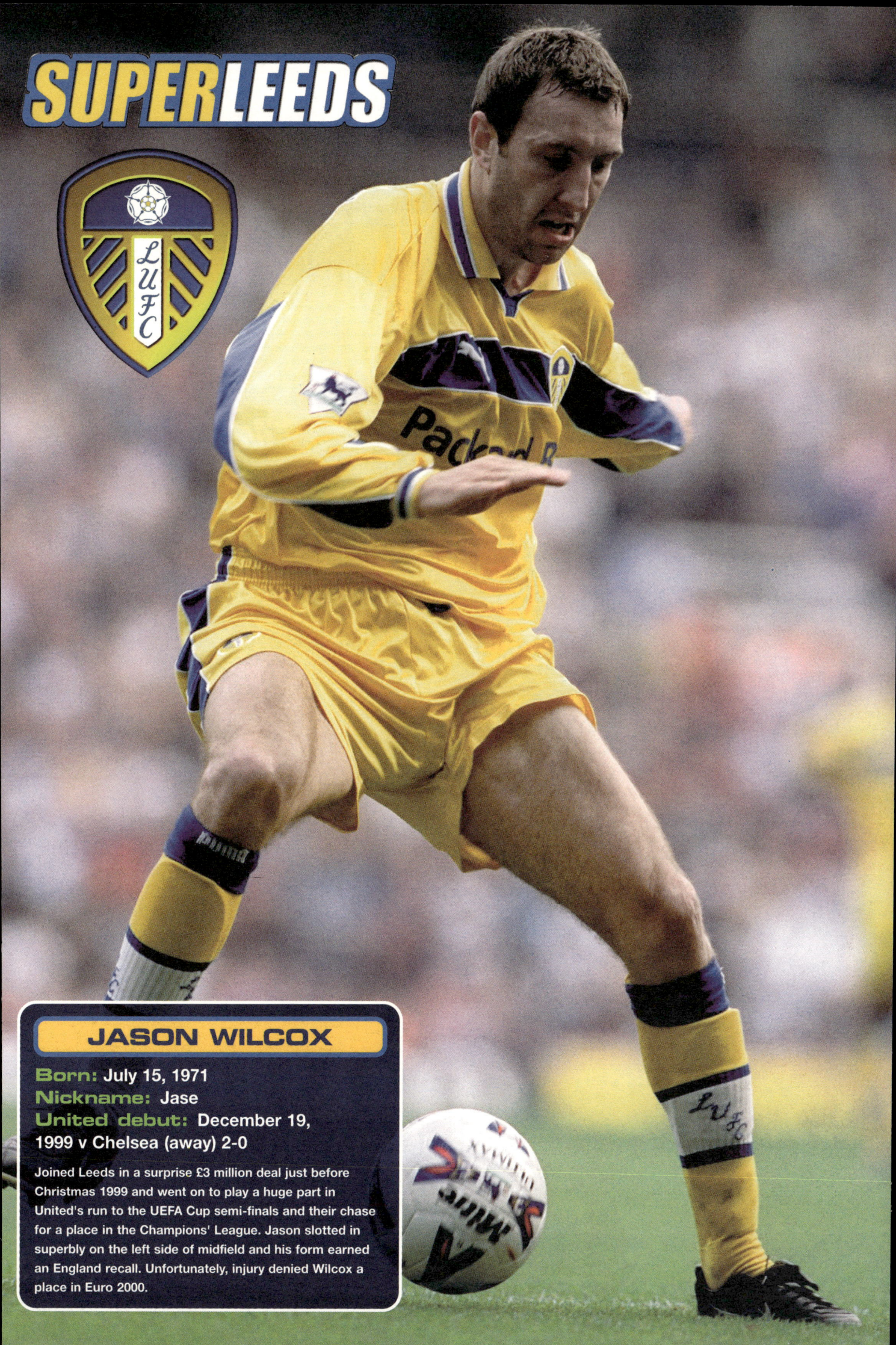

SUPERLEEDS

JASON WILCOX

Born: July 15, 1971
Nickname: Jase
United debut: December 19, 1999 v Chelsea (away) 2-0

Joined Leeds in a surprise £3 million deal just before Christmas 1999 and went on to play a huge part in United's run to the UEFA Cup semi-finals and their chase for a place in the Champions' League. Jason slotted in superbly on the left side of midfield and his form earned an England recall. Unfortunately, injury denied Wilcox a place in Euro 2000.

Leeds Legends

Paul Madeley:

Played in every position for Leeds except goalkeeper in a 17-year career at Elland Road. Leeds had a reputation as a 'hard' team in the 1960 and 70s, but Madeley was booked just twice in more than 700 games which brought him a host of medals during United's Glory Days. He won 24 England caps before retiring in 1980 and becoming a successful businessman.

Joe Jordan:

Signed for £15,000 from Morton in 1970 after playing only a handful of games in Scotland, Jordan was confined to the bench in his early days at Elland Road. However he was gradually transformed into an inspirational leader of the United attack and won a championship medal in 1974. Capped by Scotland 52 times, Jordan moved to Manchester United for a then record fee of £350,000 in 1978.

Terry Cooper:

Will always have a special place in United's history for scoring the winning goal when the club lifted its first major trophy. Cooper netted the winner in a 1-0 victory over Arsenal at Wembley in 1968 to lift the League Cup. He made his debut on the day Leeds gained promotion to the First Division in 1964 and went on to become a superb full back with a devastating burst of pace which meant he was an invaluable attacking threat. Capped 20 times by England.

John Charles:

Possibly the greatest ever Leeds United player. 'Big John' signed for Leeds on his 16th birthday and within three months had made his debut in the first team. He started his career as a defender and virtually no-one could get past him. 'Big John' then switched to centre forward and did superbly, scoring 42 league goals in the 1953-54 season - a total which is unlikely ever to be beaten. He went on to become an equally legendary figure in Italy after spells with Juventus and Roma and was even voted Footballer of the Year over there.

SL 2000 PAGE 29

DID YOU KNOW?
ODD UNITED FACTS THAT ARE STRANGE BUT TRUE

UNIQUE HAT-TRICK

South African striker Phil Masinga grabbed a unique hat-trick for Leeds United in January 1995.

United have netted nearly 100 hat-tricks in all competitions but Masinga is the only one to grab all three in extra-time of a game after coming on as a substitute.

Masinga, who joined United at the same time as current skipper Lucas Radebe, grabbed the match-ball in a 5-2 FA Cup victory over Walsall at Elland Road.

YET TO VISIT

Leeds United are yet to visit several clubs in the Premiership and Football League.

These are Southend United, Wycombe Wanderers, Crewe Alexandra, Kidderminster Harriers, Macclesfield, Cheltenham Town and Barnet. United have played just friendly games at both Wrexham and Tranmere Rovers.

LOWEST CROWD

The lowest crowd to watch a United league game came at Wimbledon's old Plough Lane ground when just 3,492 watched a 3-0 in December 1985. The United goals came from Ian Snodin, Ian Baird and Martin Dickinson.

Shortest reign as Leeds Boss

Brian Clough may have gone on to lift the European Cup with Nottingham Forest and proved himself to be one of the greatest managers of all time, but he was sacked by Leeds just 44 days after taking charge.

The charismatic Clough had the enviable task of trying to replace the legendary Don Revie who had moved on to take charge of England in the summer of 1974. Leeds were a great side in those days and had just lifted the league title for the second time when Clough, a fierce critic of that United side, was appointed.

He had impressed as a young manager at Hartlepool before going on to help steer Derby County to the championship. However rumours of unrest in the dressing room started seeping out of Elland Road very quickly and after some early disappointing results, Clough was sacked after just 44 days.

That makes his the shortest reign of any boss at Elland Road although Jock Stein lasted just one day longer in 1978. However he decided to leave United after being offered the Scotland manager's job.

Clough put his experience at Elland Road behind him and went on to turn Second Division Nottingham Forest into the best side in Europe for two years running. He retired in 1993.

Fewest Goals

United's lowest ever goals tally came in the 1996-97 Premiership season when they bagged just 28 in 38 league games.

It was the season George Graham replaced Howard Wilkinson as boss and the former Arsenal manager attempted to stabilise the United side by concentrating on defence. United figured in nine goalless draws and eventually finished 11th

The previous lowest tally was 39 which United achieved in the 1980-81 and 1981-82 seasons although both times they played 42 league games. The latter season saw Leeds relegated from the old First Division.

DON'S RECORD-BREAKING RUN

United's longest unbeaten run at home in the league was 39 games which ran from August 1968 to February 1970.

It was during a golden time for United as Don Revie's men matured into a wonderful team and the start of the fine run at Elland Road coincided with the club's title triumph in 1968-69 season.

That was an amazing campaign for United because the 5-1 defeat at Burnley's Turf Moor on October 19 was the last time United lost a league game. Of the remaining 28 fixtures, Revie's side won 17 and drew 11 with seven of those victories being in consecutive games.

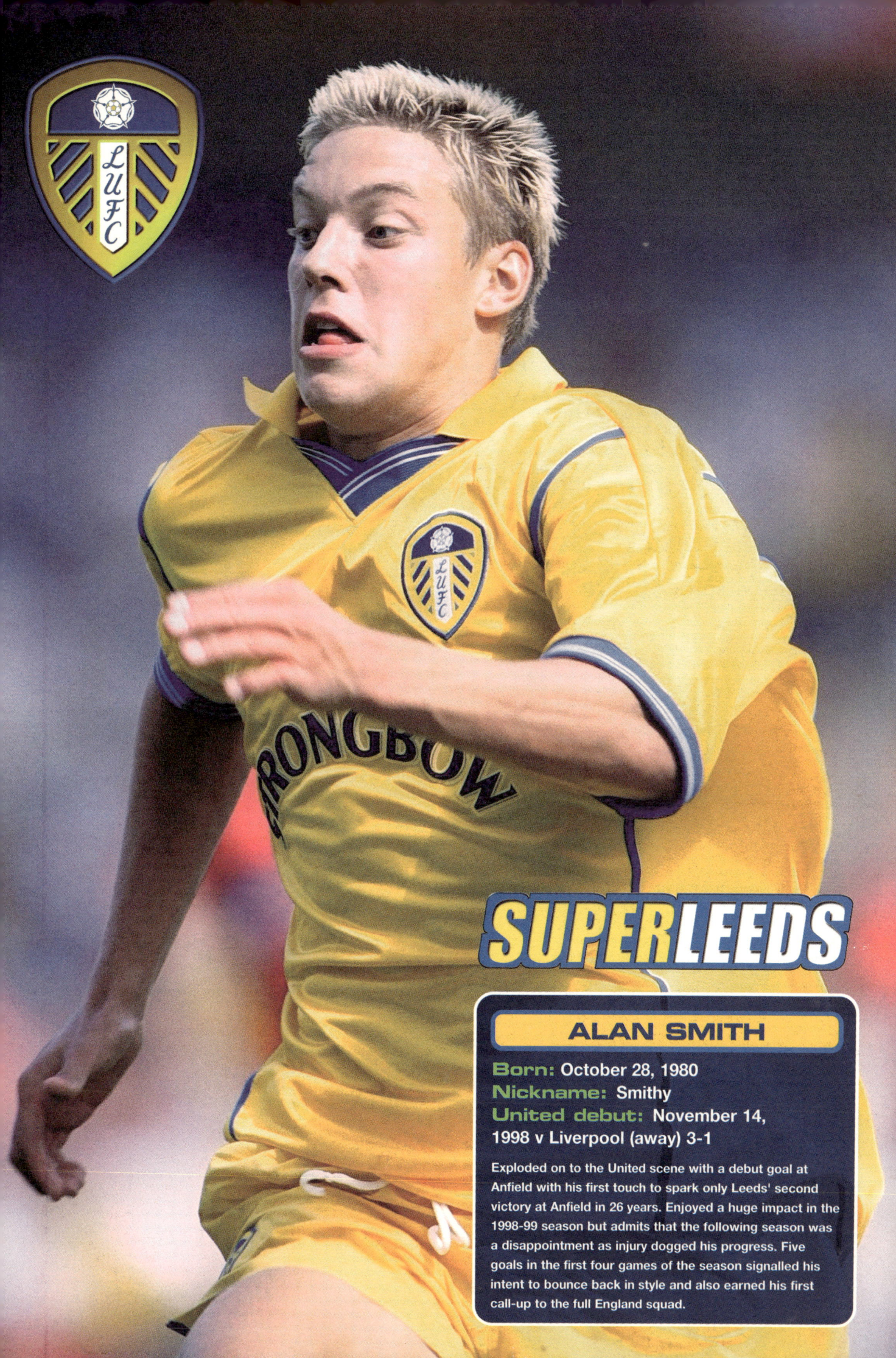

SUPERLEEDS

ALAN SMITH

Born: October 28, 1980
Nickname: Smithy
United debut: November 14, 1998 v Liverpool (away) 3-1

Exploded on to the United scene with a debut goal at Anfield with his first touch to spark only Leeds' second victory at Anfield in 26 years. Enjoyed a huge impact in the 1998-99 season but admits that the following season was a disappointment as injury dogged his progress. Five goals in the first four games of the season signalled his intent to bounce back in style and also earned his first call-up to the full England squad.

When Leeds won promotion in 1990 to end an eight-year spell outside the top flight, few could imagine the impact Howard Wilkinson's side would enjoy once back among the elite.
In their first season back, United finished a commendable fourth but this was merely a taster for what lay ahead. Leeds were neck and neck with rivals Manchester United at the top of the old First Division for much of the 1991-92 season.

However when it mattered the most, Leeds delivered and victory at Sheffield United in the penultimate game was enough to clinch the title. It was a day no Leeds fan will ever want to forget as a 3-2 triumph coupled with Manchester United's 2-0 defeat at Liverpool prompted party scenes all over the city.
It was a deserved reward for a magnificent season with Gordon Strachan, Lee Chapman, Gary McAllister and their team-mates proving they were number one by being crowned champions for the third time in the club's history.

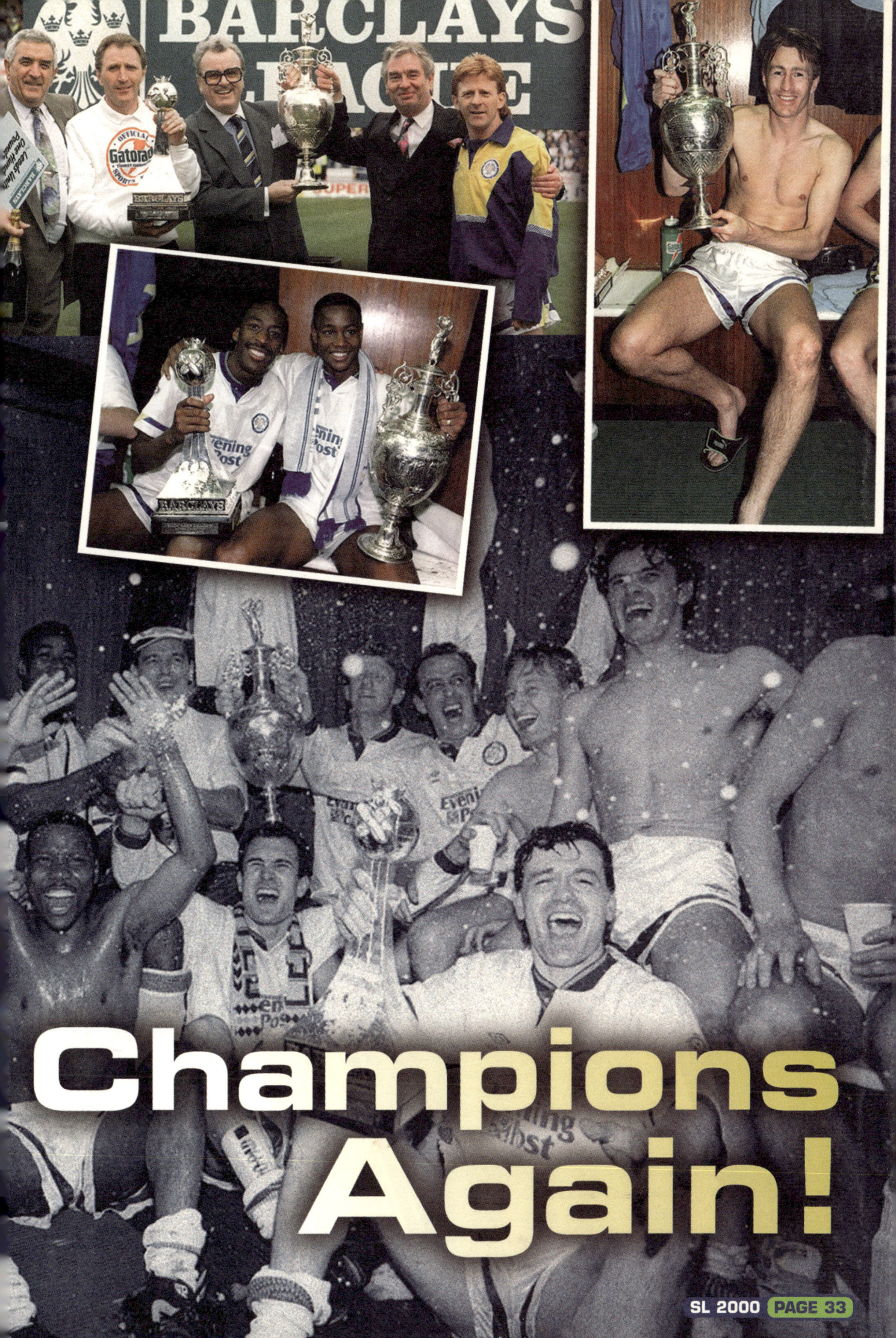

Dragon Set To Roar

It's not been a good few years for Welsh football. Back in 1993 they were 27th in the world according to the official Fifa ratings. At the start of the new Millennium they were 113th, behind countries like Azerbaijan, Oman, Cuba and Vietnam, who hardly spring to mind when football is spoken of.

But Leeds' midfielder Matthew Jones thinks his country's fortunes are about to change as manager Mark Hughes puts together a squad of young players and tries to rebuild the Principality's shattered football image.

There's no doubting Matthew's passion for his home land. His Mitsubishi Shogun four-wheel drive is in Wales red, and his mobile phone carries the green dragon symbol. And the lad, who grew up in Llanelli and won his first full cap against Qatar when he was only 19, is certain the next generation of footballers will have the valleys singing again.

He said: "The improvement has been happening for some time now but it's a long process. It's like what happened at Leeds United where we've been together from the age of 16, and a year or two down the line you can see some progress. That's what I think is happening with Wales. It's going to take a bit longer because we're not together every day of the week but when we do meet up, you can sense something is happening.

"Like David O'Leary, Mark Hughes has shown that he's not afraid to put young players in the team and let them show people what they can do, and we've got some good young players coming through."

Matthew is convinced that in former Manchester United, Barcelona, Chelsea, Southampton and Everton striker Hughes, who won 72 caps for his country, Wales have a manager who can instil in the team the heart and spirit, which many critics have felt has been missing in recent years. His presence has already seen talented players like Manchester United winger Ryan Giggs renew their enthusiasm for pulling on the scarlet shirt.

Jones adds: "Mark Hughes died for his country when he was playing. He has a real passion for Welsh football and he's more frustrated than anyone else that success has been so limited. He's starting to turn a lot of things round and there couldn't be a better person to be in charge.

"All the players have a lot of respect for the manager and he shows us respect in return. That's vital and that's stood out for me while I've been with the squad."

Already Hughes has shown enormous trust in the hard-tackling midfielder who was part of Leeds' double winning youth team alongside Harry Kewell, Jonathan Woodgate, Stephen McPhail and Paul Robinson. When Wales played Brazil and Portugal in the summer, Matthew was asked to do a marking job on World Footballer of the year Rivaldo, and Luis Figo, the most expensive player in the world. And he came out of the clashes with a lot of credit.

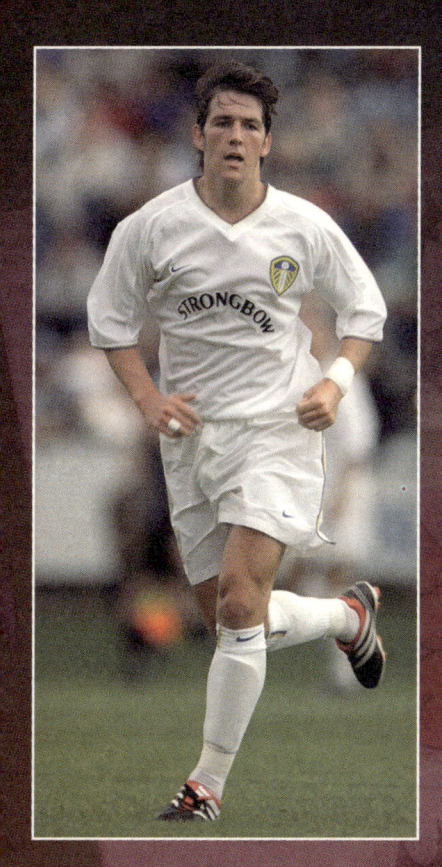

"Matthew is a great prospect," Hughes declared. "He has a great chance. He's a strong character whose ability is not in question, so if he plays to his potential, there will be a lot of full Wales caps ahead of him."

With that appearance against Qatar, Matthew has now played for Wales at every level and he's captained every team except the first team. He's hoping to complete the set one day.

"I would love to captain Wales. It's all about learning and because international matches don't come as often as club matches, it's important to play in as many as you can. It would make history and be the culmination of an ambition.

"I was proud when I became the youngest player to play for Wales at under-21 and then captained them at 18. I know there are people like Gary Speed and others that are ahead of me but it remains an ambition. For now I want to keep playing as often as possible so that I can become a young but very experienced player and then one day hopefully I'll get the armband."

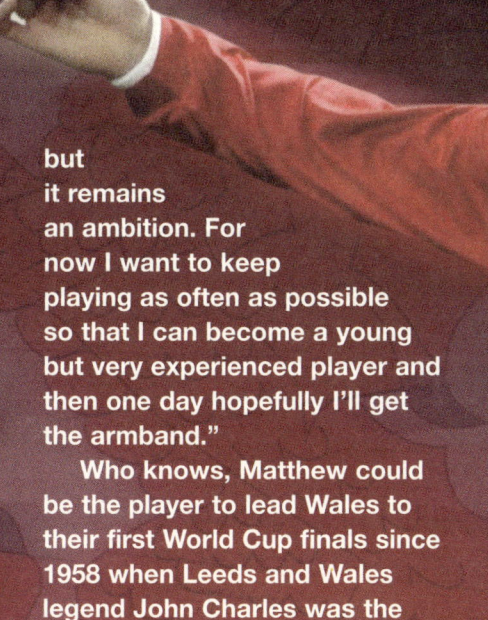

Who knows, Matthew could be the player to lead Wales to their first World Cup finals since 1958 when Leeds and Wales legend John Charles was the star.

SL 2000 PAGE 35

UNITED COUNTRIES

MATCH THE LEEDS UNITED INTERNATIONAL STARS WITH THEIR NATIONAL FLAGS

Quick Quiz

1. Who holds the record for most appearances for Leeds United?
2. Which club did United sign Dominic Matteo from earlier this season?
3. Which two Leeds players appeared for Australia in the 2000 Olympics?
4. Who did Leeds United knock out of the Champions League qualifiers this season?
5. What was the fee Leeds paid Lens for midfielder Olivier Dacourt this summer?
6. Which Premiership club do former Leeds strikers Brian Deane and Noel Whelan play for?
7. Who captained Leeds United to their last league championship winning season in 1991-92?
8. What is the record crowd at Elland Road for a Leeds match?
9. Which club did David O'Leary spend the majority of his playing career with?
10. How many times have Leeds United won the FA Cup?

Number Fun

USE UNITED'S SQUAD NUMBERS TO WORK OUT WHO THE MYSTERY PLAYER IS

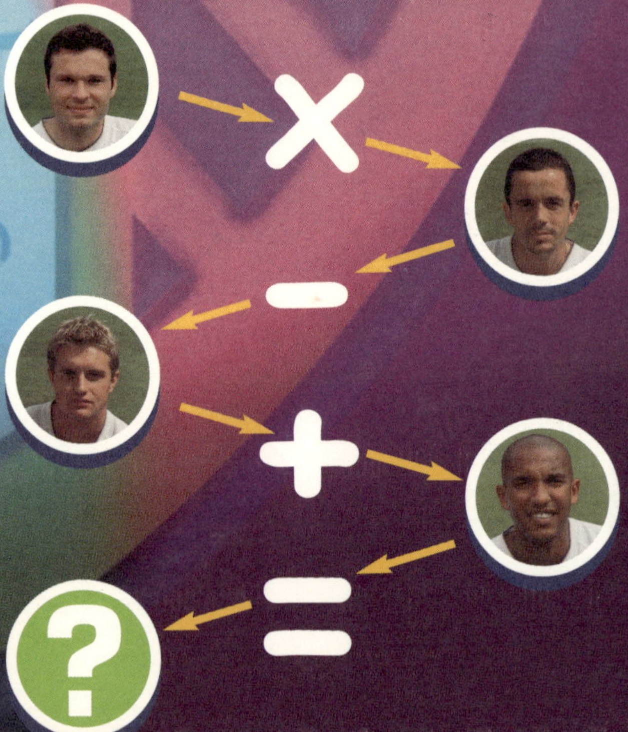

YOU CAN FIND THE ANSWERS TO THIS AND ALL THE OTHER QUIZZES ON PAGE 48!

PAGE 36 SL 2000

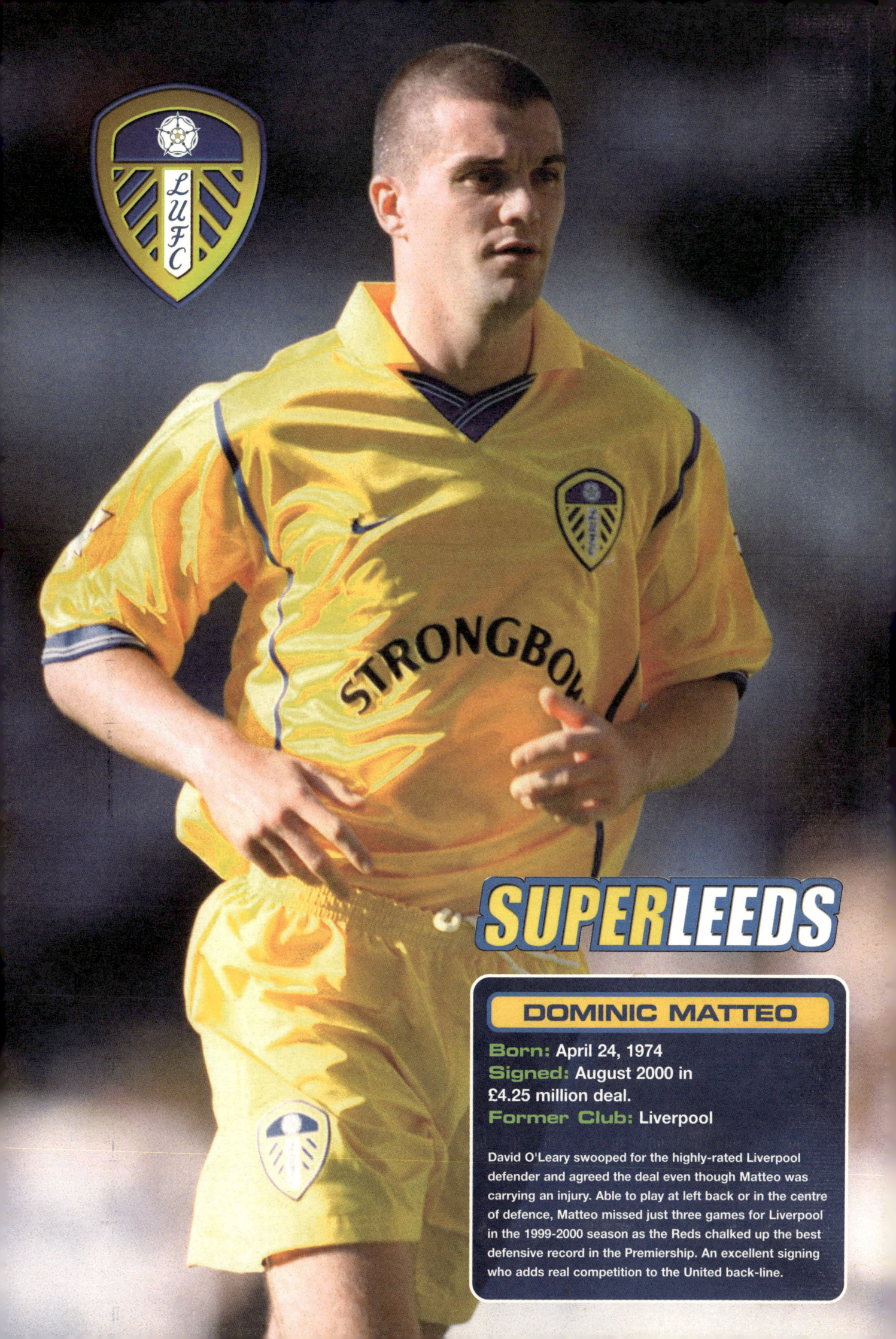

SUPERLEEDS

DOMINIC MATTEO

Born: April 24, 1974
Signed: August 2000 in £4.25 million deal.
Former Club: Liverpool

David O'Leary swooped for the highly-rated Liverpool defender and agreed the deal even though Matteo was carrying an injury. Able to play at left back or in the centre of defence, Matteo missed just three games for Liverpool in the 1999-2000 season as the Reds chalked up the best defensive record in the Premiership. An excellent signing who adds real competition to the United back-line.

PLAY LIKE

If you want to be a better footballer, you can learn a lot by watching football, live or on TV, or even by studying photographs in the newspapers and magazines.

Football in the Community coach, Andrea Loberto, whose coaching hints appear each month in Super Leeds, picks out some useful tips from these photos of Leeds ace Alan Smith and gives you some drills so you can match Smithy's skills.

Alan Smith shows great skill by getting away from Barcelona's Phillipe Cocu. Smithy is in a well-balanced body position and keeps the ball under close control. While he keeps his eyes on the ball he is aware of space and defenders around him. After changing direction Smithy accelerates away leaving the Barcelona defenders in his wake and uses his body to protect the ball.

Exercise One

In a 10 by 10 area each player has a ball. Taking it in turn, one player is the tagger and in one minute tries to tag the other player as many times as possible. The other player is trying to keep away from the tagger. Both players must stay inside the area. The tagger must have the ball under control all the time. After one minute swap the players. The player with the most points is the winner.

Exercise Two

Have two servers who take it in turn to pass the ball to the attacker who tries to score past the goalkeeper. Make sure that the attacker shoots with both feet. Emphasise accuracy before power. Have the attackers shoot first time and also have the servers become defenders once they pass the ball.

SMITHY!

Alan Smith demonstrates that all good players are comfortable shooting with both feet. After having observed the goalkeeper's position Smithy keeps his eyes on the ball and lines up a shot with his left foot. Just like all good strikers Alan Smith makes sure that his shots are accurate and always on target, and always has a positive attitude. He has a good shooting technique able to score with both left and right foot, volleys, half-volleys, inside and outside the penalty area.

Exercise Three

In a 10 by 20 area players try to dribble past the opposing defender and score in either of the two goals at the opposite end. To score a goal you must dribble the ball under close control through the goals. Play for one minute and the winner is the player with the most points. Encourage players to attack space, changing direction and speed and unbalance defenders.

Viduka
Likes Making

Ask Leeds ace Mark Viduka what made him become a striker and he answers quite simply: The thrill of scoring goals.

His Mark

The Australian joined United in a £6 million deal from Scottish giants Celtic during the summer to bring some much-needed height to the Leeds front-line.

And the 25-year-old is hoping to prove as big a hit in England as he was north of the border.

Mark netted 27 goals in his only full season in Scotland and was voted Player of the Year while at Parkhead.

The big striker, who was brought up in Melbourne where Aussie Rules Football dominates, has played up front ever since first kicking a ball around.

And the Aussie star says he was never interested in playing anywhere else on a soccer field.

He said: "I have always been a striker. My dad took me to watch soccer when I was about three years old and I always liked the look of being a striker.

"When I started playing I found I just loved the feeling of scoring goals. I still do. That is why I have always been a striker and never wanted to play anywhere else."

Mark started his professional career back home in Australia with Melbourne Knights where he made a big impact and served notice as to his potential.

His first season in 1993-94 saw Mark claim 17 goals in 20 Australian National League games and he followed this with 21 goals from 24 games the following campaign as the Knights lifted the championship.

That scoring rate helped secure a move to Croatia Zagreb amid rumoured interest from Real Madrid and Borussia Dortmund. It was in Zagreb that his career really started to take off.

His first season in his parents' homeland saw Mark claim 12 goals in 27 games while the following campaign, 1996-97, was his best in Croatia with 18 goals from 25 appearances.

Mark impressed during his time with Zagreb as he helped the club become the side to beat in Croatian football.

In the 1997-98 season, his goals and all-round link play helped Zagreb clinch the league and cup double in Croatia and earn a coveted place in the Champions League the following year.

Zagreb won through to the group stages in the 1998-99 season with a 3-1 aggregate

FACT-FILE:

Born: October 9, 1975. Australia.
Position: Forward.
Leeds Debut: TSV 1860 Munich in the Champions League third round first leg qualifier. Elland Road - August 9, 2000. Leeds won 2-1
Former clubs: Melbourne Knights, Croatia Zagreb, Celtic.
International: Australia.

SL 2000 PAGE 41

"I have always been tall for my age which was a big help because it meant I played up front."

victory over Celtic and Viduka played so well that the Glasgow club soon took him to Scotland in a £3.75 million deal.

However before that move in November 1998, he managed to grab his first experience of Champions League group stages football with Zagreb.

Mark's team were handed a tough group alongside Olympiakos, Ajax and Porto and although Zagreb collected eight points from six games it was not enough to go through.

Mark said: "I enjoyed the buzz of playing Champions League football for Zagreb and it was a great experience."

After his £3.75 million deal, the Australian went on to become a huge hit at Parkhead by scoring 27 goals and winning the Player of the Year award in his only full season in Scotland.

Mark loves his job as a professional footballer and says he has never regretted choosing to be a striker.

He said: "I started playing for Melbourne Croatia in 1982 when I was about six-years-old and I started up front.

"I have always been tall for my age which was a big help because it meant I played up front."

Mark soon started to earn a reputation in junior football back home as he often scored more than 70 goals per season.

By the age of 14, Mark was being wooed by the leading National League clubs in Australia before eventually being offered a full-time soccer scholarship by the Australia Institute of Sport.

It was there that Mark really started to hone his goal-scoring skills and this led to being selected for the Under-17's World Youth Championship in Qatar.

Mark explains how he was hooked on soccer at a very early age.

He said: "In Australia, you can't have a side below the Under-9's age group so at first I was playing with boys who were three years older. I was just six but playing for the Under-9s.

"Despite that, I finished top scorer every year until I left when I was still a teenager.

"That was when I went to the Australia Institute of Sport and I stayed there for another two years before joining the Melbourne Knights.

"I was with the Knights for another two years before moving to Croatia Zagreb.

"I subsequently moved to Celtic and then Leeds. I am very happy here. It is a good team to be part of and a good club."

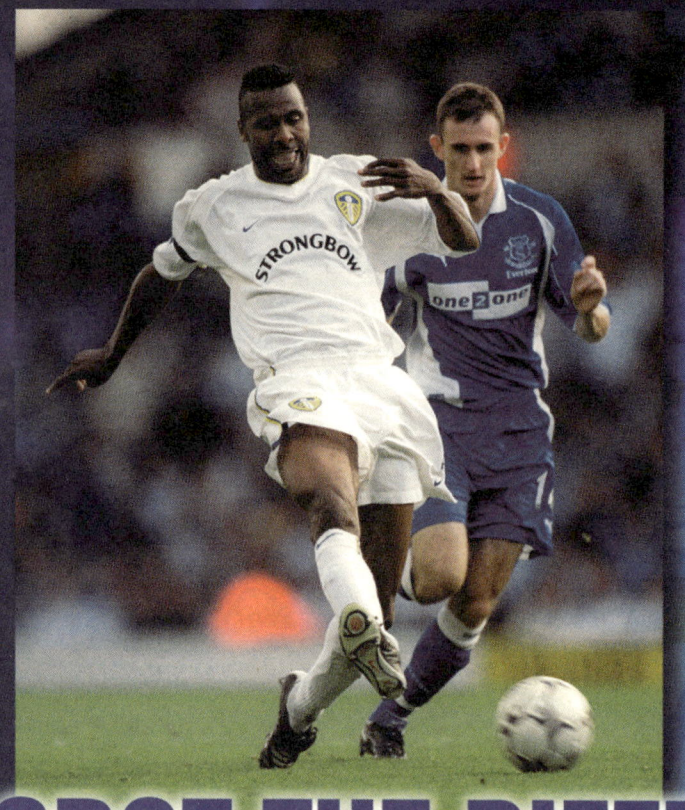

SPOT THE DIFFERENCE

Above are two near identical pictures but with ten very subtle differences, can you spot them?

NAME GAMES

Unscramble the names of five United stars

YNIANRMTGEL

LAAUARYMBNY

DIBATDTAVY

REWKAELYHRL

IMADCESIGHBREL

Who Am I?

How many clues do you need to guess who I am?

1) I was born in England and have played for the Under-21s.
2) I made my professional debut aged just 18.
3) I have been called up to the full England squad.
4) I have captained the Football League representative side.
5) I started my career at Norwich City.
6) I helped a former club win promotion to the Premiership in 1998.
7) I joined Leeds in the summer of 1999 in a £4 million deal from Charlton Athletic.
8) I haved played at right back, left back and in the centre of defence this season.

YOU CAN FIND THE ANSWERS TO THIS AND ALL THE OTHER QUIZZES ON PAGE 48!

PAGE 44 SL 2000

SUPERLEEDS

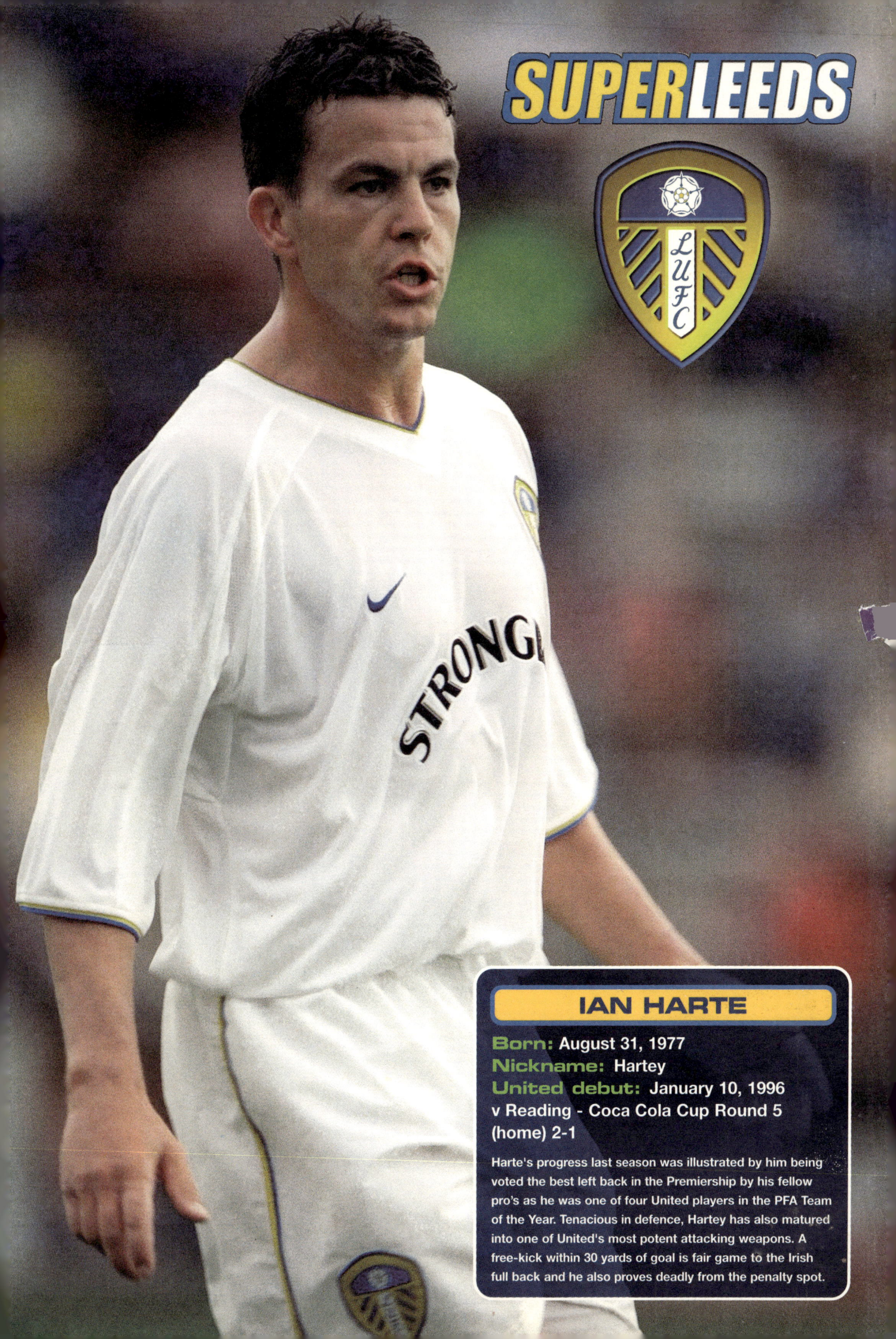

IAN HARTE

Born: August 31, 1977
Nickname: Hartey
United debut: January 10, 1996 v Reading - Coca Cola Cup Round 5 (home) 2-1

Harte's progress last season was illustrated by him being voted the best left back in the Premiership by his fellow pro's as he was one of four United players in the PFA Team of the Year. Tenacious in defence, Hartey has also matured into one of United's most potent attacking weapons. A free-kick within 30 yards of goal is fair game to the Irish full back and he also proves deadly from the penalty spot.

FUTURE IN GOOD HANDS

The men with a mission, Pop Robson and Brian Kidd have been brought to the Club to find United's future stars

Frazer Richardson - Could he be the next to make the break through?

Leeds United have quite rightly been praised for their faith in youth development at Elland Road.

While some Premiership clubs have been forced to splash millions of pounds on new signings, the Academy at Thorp Arch has provided Leeds with a host of top class players.

Any bright star of the future knows he will be given his chance at Elland Road under David O'Leary.

The likes of Harry Kewell, Stephen McPhail, Ian Harte, Alan Smith and Jonathan Woodgate have all developed into some of the most exciting talents around after joining United as young teenagers.

And a quick visit to the club's Thorp Arch training ground shows there is even more talent waiting in the wings.

Gareth Evans has already burst into the first team with his debut coming in the wonderful 1-0 victory against TSV 1860 Munich.

The left back or midfielder, who was in the same school team as Alan Smith, has an abundance of skill and gives the first team squad competition down the left flank.

Gareth has already shown in his fleeting appearances that he has the potential to become the latest to graduate to the first team from the reserves and youth team.

Midfielder Simon Watson is another who will be hoping to make progress this term after missing the final months of the previous campaign through injury.

He suffered the nightmare of a broken leg while playing in the reserve side's 1-1 draw with Blackburn Rovers in February last season. It was literally a bad break because he had been playing well in the weeks leading up to the injury.

Frazer Richardson has been on United's books for several seasons and has played in a wide variety of positions in defence and midfield.

The second year apprentice recently celebrated his 18th birthday and has made good progress with the reserve side.

United's commitment to youth development also sees them scour the globe for talented youngsters and Leeds are hoping the next star of the future will be Jacob Burns.

Signed from Australian side Parramatta Power in August for £250,000, Jacob has already been on the bench in one of the best stadiums in the world - the Nou Camp in Barcelona.

Harry Kewell and Mark Viduka have set the standard for Australians in English football and the 22-year-old left-footed midfielder is hoping to follow in their illustrious footsteps.

David Sherman is another youngster who has been making good progress with the 17-year-old with reserve team experience already under his belt.

Of course, most of the focus on a football club surrounds the first team and Leeds United are no different in that respect.

However it is reassuring for all United fans to know that the future of the club is in such good hands.

Jacob Burns is the latest Australian import

Gareth Evans - He's already tasted first team action

TRIVIA Challenge

1 - Everton.
2 - Nigel Martyn and Eirik Bakke.
3 - Celtic.
4 - Gordon Strachan.
5 - Arsenal.
6 - Brian Kidd.
7 - 69.
8 - Stephen McPhail.
9 - Alan Smith in the 2-1 home win against TSV 1860 Munich.
10 - Manchester City.

SPOT THE EURO GROUNDS

1 - This is the NOU CAMP in SPAIN and BARCELONA play here.
2 - This is the SAN SIRO in ITALY and AC MILAN play here.
3 - This is the OLYMPIC STADIUM (Rome) in ITALY and ROMA play here.
4 - This is the OLYMPIC STADIUM (Munich) in GERMANY and MUNICH 1860 play here.

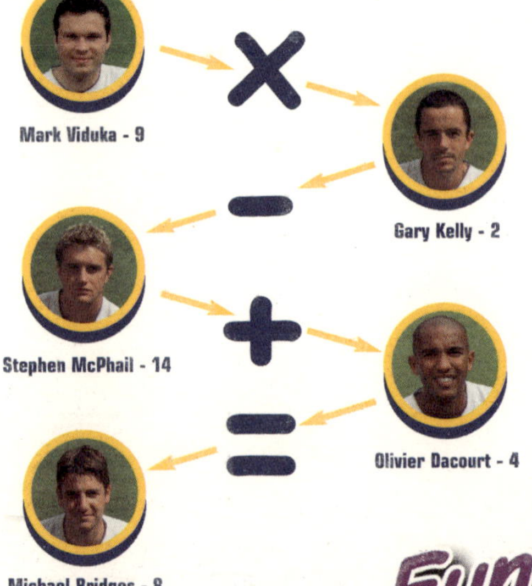

Quick Quiz

1 - Jack Charlton played 773 times for Leeds.
2 - Liverpool.
3 - Mark Viduka and Danny Milosevic
4 - TSV 1860 Munich.
5 - £7.2 million.
6 - Middlesbrough.
7 - Gordon Strachan
8 - 57,892 v Sunderland in FA Cup. 1967.
9 - Arsenal.
10 - Once (1972 v Arsenal).

SUPERLEEDS QUIZ SOLUTIONS

UNITED COUNTRIES

NAME GAMES

YNIANRMTGEL - NIGEL MARTYN
LAAUARYMBNY - ALAN MAYBURY
DIBATDTAVY - DAVID BATTY
REWKAELYHRL - HARRY KEWELL
IMADCESIGHBREL - MICHAEL BRIDGES

SPOT THE DIFFERENCE

Who Am I?
Answer - DANNY MILLS

Number Fun

Mark Viduka - 9
Gary Kelly - 2
Stephen McPhail - 14
Olivier Dacourt - 4
Michael Bridges - 8

SL 2000 PAGE 48

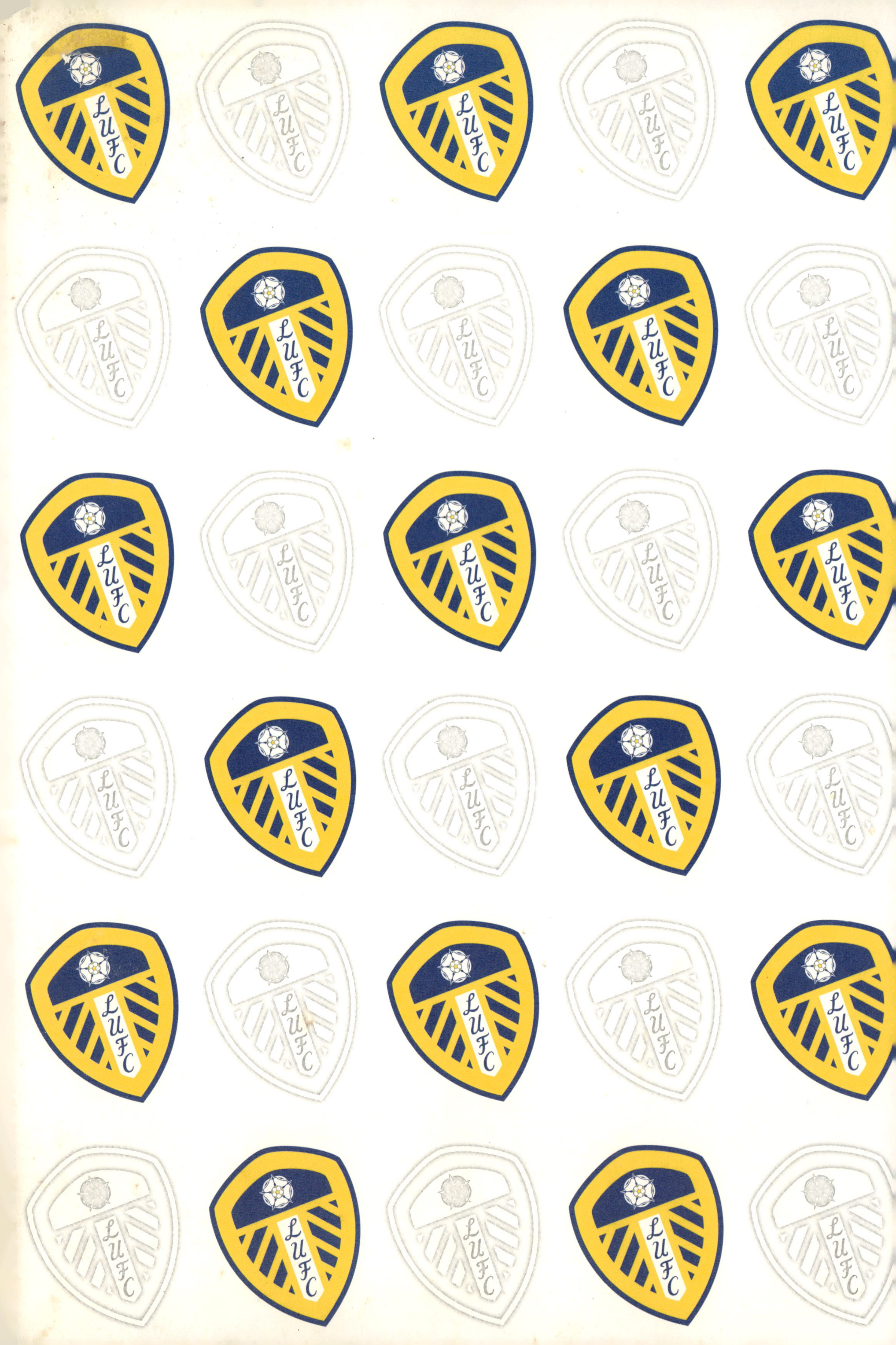
LUFC